This

Easy Recipes With Fresh Herbs

Belongs to:

_____

"You are a seed dropping from above
To be nurtured by earth
And to grow into a healing herb
For the whole world to consume."
— Michael Bassey Johnson

Copyright © 2022 www.the-crest.co.uk W.H.I.F. Publishing

Cooking Measure Conversions

DRY WEIGHTS

1/2 oz	1 tbsp	–	15 g
1 oz	2 tbsp	1/8 c	28 g
2 oz	4 tbsp	1/4 c	57 g
3 oz	6 tbsp	1/3 c	85 g
4 oz	8 tbsp	1/2 c	115 g
8 oz	16 tbsp	1 cup	227 g
12 oz	24 tbsp	1½ c	340 g
16 oz	32 tbsp	2 c	455 g

1 OZ = 28 GRAMS
1 LBS = 454 G
1 CUP = 227 G

1 TSP = 5 ML
1 TBSP = 15 ML
1 OZ = 30 ML
1 CUP = 237 ML
1 PINT = 473 ML (2 CUPS)
1 GALLON = 16 CUPS

LIQUID VOLUMES

1 oz	2 tbsp	1/8 c	30 ml
2 oz	4 tbsp	1/4 c	60 ml
2⅔ oz	6 tbsp	1/3 c	80 ml
4 oz	8 tbsp	1/2 c	120 ml
8 oz	16 tbsp	2/3 c	160 ml
12 oz	24 tbsp	3/4 c	177 ml
16 oz	32 tbsp	1 cup	237 ml
32 oz	64 tbsp	1½ c	470 ml
		2 c	950 ml

ABBREVIATIONS

tbsp = Tablespoon
tsp = Teaspoon
fl.oz = Fluid Ounce
c = cup
ml = Milliliter
lb = pound
F = Fahrenheit
C = Celsius
ml = Milliliter
g = grams
kg = kilogram
l = liter

BAKING PAN

9-inch (by 3") standard round pan = 12 cups
9-inch (by 2.5") springform pan = 10 cups
10-inch (by 4") tube pan = 16 cups
9-inch (by 3") bundt pan = 12 cups
9-inch (by 2") square pan = 10 cups
9 x 5 inch loaf pan = 8 cups

OVEN TEMP.

130 c = 250 F
165 c = 325 F
177 c = 350 F
190 c = 375 F
200 c = 400 F
220 c = 425 F

Copyright © 2022 www.the-crest.co.uk W.H.I.F. Publishing
All rights reserved. No part of this publication may be reproduced, distributed or transmitted in any form.

Index

	Page
1. Dill	5
2. Fennel	9
3. Parsley	13
4. Coriander	17
5. Basil	21
6. Rosemary	25
7. Chives	29
8. Garlic Chives	33
9. Lavender	37
10. Marjoram	41
11. Origanum	45
12. Thyme	49
13. Mint	53
14. Sage	57
15. Tarragon	61
List of Recipes	65

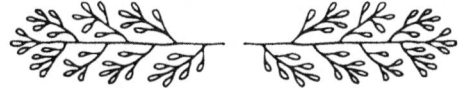

Notes

1. Dill

Dill is a versatile herb that can be used in a variety of dishes, such as in a potato salad, tzatziki sauce, or over fish. Dill seeds can be used as a spice to flavour foods like pickles or bread. Because it has such a unique taste, a small amount of dill can go a long way, which is why dill is so good to use as a garnish. The feathery texture of dill leaves looks beautiful, and a small sprig of dill can add a noticeable aroma to a dish.

When used in cooking, dill weed will lose flavour the longer it is cooked, so it should be added at the last minute only. The opposite is true for dill seed, which develops more aroma and flavour when heated. Recipes often call dill seed to be toasted in a hot frying pan before being added. As well, dill seeds are often used in pickling.

Potato Salad with Dill

Ingredients
3 pounds baby potatoes
1/4 cup minced shallot/onion (about 1 large)
1/4 cup fresh dill, minced
2 tablespoons fresh parsley
1/4 cup white wine vinegar
1 teaspoon salt
1/4 cup capers, drained
2 tablespoons olive oil
Fresh ground pepper

Instructions
- Fill a large pot with cold water and add 1 tablespoon salt. Add the whole potatoes and bring to a boil, boil for about 5 to 8 minutes, depending on the size. Cook until fork tender (taste test to check).
- Mince the shallot/onion. Finely chop the dill and parsley.
- When the potatoes are done, drain them. When they are cool enough to handle, slice them into bite sized pieces. Place the potatoes in a bowl and gently mix in the minced shallot, white wine vinegar, kosher salt, and 1/2 cup warm water. Let stand for 5 minutes, gently stirring occasionally. The potatoes will absorb the water as they stand.
- Add the dill, parsley, drained capers, olive oil, and a few grinds black pepper. Taste and add additional salt if necessary (we added 1/4 teaspoon more). Serve warm or room temperature.

Dill Pickles

Ingredients
2 x 1-pint wide-mouth mason jars with lids
1.5 to 2 pounds small cucumbers
3 cloves garlic
½ tablespoon coriander seeds
1 tablespoon whole peppercorns
1 tablespoon salt
½ tablespoon sugar
2/3 cup white vinegar
1 ⅓ cup water
1 large handful fresh dill (or 2 teaspoons dill seeds)

Instructions
Wash two mason jars and lids in hot soapy water, rinse, and let air dry.
Quarter the cucumbers into four slices lengthwise to fit into the jars. Peel and cut the garlic cloves in half.
In a saucepan, place the coriander seeds, whole peppercorns, sugar, salt, white vinegar, and water. Whisk over low heat until fully dissolved, then remove from the heat.
In the two clean mason jars, tightly pack the cucumbers, garlic, and fresh dill.
Pour the brine mixture over the cucumbers. Tap the jars on the counter to release any air bubbles and top off the jar with extra water if any cucumbers are exposed.
Place the lids on the jars and screw on the rings until they are hand tight.
For refrigerator pickles: Leave the jars in the fridge for 24 hours before tasting. The pickles last up to 1 month in the refrigerator.

Notes

2. Fennel

Fennel is a highly aromatic and flavourful herb and is a member of the carrot family, though it's not a root vegetable. The base of its long stalks weaves together to form a thick, crisp bulb that grows above ground. Above the bulb, at the tip of the stalks, it has light, feathery leaves that resemble dill. When it goes to seed, fennel also produces small yellow flowers among the leaves. Every part of it is edible, from the bulb to the flowers, and it can be eaten raw or cooked.

Fennel stalks can take the place of celery in soups and stews and can be used as a "bed" for roasted chicken and meats. Use fennel fronds as a garnish or chop them and use as you would other herbs, like dill or parsley. Fennel and seafood also go together like peas in a pod.

Creamy Pasta with Fennel, Spring Onions, and Bacon

Ingredients

6 slices (about 6 ounces; 170g) thick-cut bacon
1 pound (450g) spring onions, trimmed, white and green parts divided and thinly sliced
1 fennel bulb (about 1 pound; 450g), cored and thinly sliced, fronds reserved
1/4 cup (60ml) water
Salt
1/8 teaspoon baking soda
1 cup (235ml) heavy cream
1 pound (450g) dried pasta
Freshly ground black pepper
1 cup (about 3 ounces; 85g) grated Parmesan

Instructions

- Cook bacon over medium-low heat until crispy. Using tongs, transfer bacon to a cutting board and reserve rendered bacon fat in the pan. Cut bacon crosswise into 3/4-inch pieces; set aside.
- Return pan to stovetop and increase heat and add white and light green spring onion parts, fennel, and water, season with salt and cook, stirring frequently with a rubber spatula, until vegetables just begin to soften. Add baking soda, stir to combine, and continue to cook until vegetables are very soft and beginning to break down.
- Add remaining green parts of spring onions. Cook until well-incorporated with vegetable mixture and just beginning to soften. Add cream, bring to a simmer, and cook until mixture is slightly thickened.
- Transfer mixture to a blender and blend on high speed until smooth and emulsified. Season lightly with salt. Wipe out sauté pan and transfer blended sauce back to the pan, passing through a fine-mesh strainer if desired. Warm sauce over low heat, occasionally scraping down the sides of the pan to prevent skin from forming.
- Meanwhile, in a pot of salted boiling water, cook pasta until just shy of al dente. Reserve pasta cooking water.
- Transfer pasta to pan along with 1/2 cup pasta water and bacon, increase heat to high, and cook, stirring rapidly until sauce has thickened slightly and pasta is well-coated. Remove from heat, season generously with pepper, add Parmesan, and stir rapidly to combine. Season with salt, if needed. Divide pasta into serving bowls and garnish with reserved fennel fronds. Serve immediately.

Fennel Frond Pesto with Anchovies

Fronds are those cute frilly green leafy things attached to the stalks that grow out of a fennel bulb. They kind of look like fresh dill, and they have a texture that's light and feathery.

Ingredients
1 quart lightly packed fennel fronds and tender stems (from about 4 bulbs), very roughly chopped
5 oil-packed anchovy fillets
4 medium cloves garlic
1 tablespoon Dijon mustard
Juice and zest of 1 lemon
Extra-virgin olive oil
Kosher salt

Instructions
- In a blender jar or using an immersion blender, combine fennel fronds, anchovies, garlic, mustard, and lemon juice and zest. Add enough olive oil to just barely come to the top of the solid ingredients.

- Blend until a smooth sauce forms. Season with salt to taste. Use right away, or transfer to an airtight container and refrigerate for up to 5 days.

Notes

3. Parsley

Put chopped parsley on everything: Don't chop it too finely — bigger pieces are prettier and have more flavour. Add it on top of grilled vegetables, roasted potatoes, a cold green-bean salad, stews, soups, pasta, hot or cold grain dishes like couscous or quinoa, etc.

The herb is rich in many vitamins, particularly vitamin K, which is needed for blood clotting and bone health. Parsley is also a great source of vitamins A and C — important nutrients with antioxidant properties.

Packed with flavour and low in calories!

Pomegranate and Parsley Salad

Ingredients

flat-leaf parsley a large bunch, leaves picked
rocket 90g
shallot 1 long, peeled and thinly sliced into rings
pomegranate seeds 50g

DRESSING
extra-virgin olive oil 2 tbsp
pomegranate molasses 3 tbsp
lemon 1, juiced

Instructions

- Make the dressing by whisking together the oil, molasses, and lemon juice with a little seasoning.

- Fill a large bowl with iced water and add the parsley leaves, rocket, and shallot rings. This will make them fresh, vibrant, and crunchy. Leave for 10 minutes, then drain well.

- Tip the drained salad into a bowl and toss with the dressing, then tip onto a serving plate and scatter with the pomegranate seeds to serve.

Easy Potato Tortilla with Parsley and Chorizo

Ingredients
potatoes 2 medium, peeled and thinly sliced
olive oil
onion 1, sliced
chorizo 50g, chopped
eggs 4, beaten
parsley ½ a bunch, chopped

Instructions
- Heat a pan of boiling salted water and cook the potatoes until just tender. Drain well. Heat a tbsp of olive oil in a small non-stick frying pan and cook the onion until softened. Add the chorizo and cook for a few minutes then stir in the parsley.

- Beat the eggs in a large bowl and season well. Tip the potatoes, onion and chorizo into the bowl then mix and stir.

- Wipe out the frying pan then add a tbsp more oil and heat again. Tip in the egg mix and leave over a medium heat until the bottom is browned, and the top is set. Flip the tortilla onto a plate then slide the uncooked side down back into the pan. Cook for another 5 minutes until the bottom is set.

Notes

4. Coriander

Coriander is a spice produced from the round, tan-coloured seeds of the coriander plant (Coriandrum sativum), and is related to parsley, carrots, and celery.

As a spice, the lemony and floral flavour of coriander finds its way into the many Asian, Latin, and Indian dishes, as well as European cuisine. Many people use coriander in dishes like soups and salsas. While the leaves of the coriander plant are an herb known as cilantro or Chinese parsley, the round seeds are used to make coriander spice.

Coriander leaves are often used whole, whereas the seeds are used dried or ground.

Green chutney

(Coriander, chilli, and mint)
− delicious with naan bread

Ingredients

100g coriander

50g mint

1 green chilli, finely chopped

thumb-sized piece ginger, grated

1 ½ tbsp yogurt

½ lemon, juiced

2 tsp sugar

30ml olive oil

1 tsp chaat masala

Instructions

- Put all the ingredients in a blender and blend until smooth. Do not blend for too long, otherwise it will become very dark. Season with salt to taste.

Lemon and coriander couscous

Ingredients
250g couscous
grated zest of a lemon
2 x 20g packs fresh coriander
4 tbsp raisins
4 tbsp toasted pine nuts

Instructions
- Prepare 250g couscous with boiling water or stock, according to the packet's instructions.

- Add the lemon zest, fresh coriander, raisins, and pine nuts. Season well and drizzle with plenty of olive oil. Goes well with fish or lamb.

Notes

5. Basil

Basil is an annual herb that is most often green in colour. It has a fragrant, sweet smell and peppery taste. The most common use of basil is for cooking, and it is a well-known culinary herb that's popular in many Mediterranean, and particularly Italian, cuisines.

It forms the basis of pesto and adds a distinctive flavour to salads, pasta, pizza, and other dishes. Indonesian, Thai, and Vietnamese cuisines also feature this herb.

There are over 60 varieties of basil, some of which are red or purple, and each has its own distinct flavour. Sweet basil (Ocimum basilicum) is the most popular and common variety.

Basil and Lentil Salad

Ingredients
1 1/2 cups green lentils, rinsed
3/4 tsp. kosher salt, divided, plus more
1 1/3 cups plain Greek yogurt
2 garlic cloves, finely chopped
1/2 tsp. ground turmeric
Freshly ground black pepper
1 cup unsalted, roasted sunflower seeds
1 Tbsp. plus 1 1/2 tsp. fresh lemon juice
3 Tbsp. extra-virgin olive oil, plus more for drizzling
1 ripe avocado, cut into cubes
1 cup baby rocket
1 cup basil leaves, torn if large

Instructions

- Cook lentils in a large saucepan of simmering salted water until they are tender but still retain their shape, 20–30 minutes. Drain, rinse under cold running water, and drain well again.

- Mix yogurt, garlic, turmeric, 1/4 tsp. salt, and a generous grind of pepper in a small bowl to combine; set aside.

- Toss lentils, sunflower seeds, lemon juice, 3 Tbsp. oil, and remaining 1/2 tsp. salt in a large bowl. Gently fold in avocado, rocket, and basil.

- Spread reserved yogurt sauce across a platter and spoon lentil mixture on top, drizzle with oil.

Tuna and Green Bean Salad with Basil Dressing

Ingredients

1 shallot, coarsely chopped
3 Tbsp. sherry vinegar or red wine vinegar
1 tsp. kosher salt, plus more
1 lb. green beans, trimmed
1 1/2 cups basil leaves
6 Tbsp. extra-virgin olive oil
2 Tbsp. fresh lemon juice
1 tsp. freshly ground black pepper
1 large or 2 small heads of Little Gem lettuce or romaine hearts, leaves separated
1 (14.5-oz.) can white beans, drained, rinsed
1 cup parsley leaves with tender stems
1/4 cup capers, drained
1 (6-oz.) jar oil-packed tuna, drained, flaked into pieces

Instructions

- Combine shallot, vinegar, and 1 tsp. salt in a blender jar. Let sit 5–10 minutes to lightly pickle.

- Meanwhile, cook green beans in a large pot of boiling salted water until crisp-tender, about 4 minutes. Drain, then run under very cold water until cool to the touch.

- Add basil, oil, lemon juice, and pepper to shallot mixture and blend until mostly smooth. Pour dressing into a large bowl. Add green beans, lettuce, white beans, parsley, and capers and toss with your hands to coat. Add tuna and gently toss to combine. Transfer salad to a platter.

Notes

6. Rosemary

Rosemary is a shrub with fragrant, evergreen, needle-like leaves and white, pink, purple, or blue flowers, native to the Mediterranean region.

Rosemary is an aromatic herb that is used as a flavouring in a variety of dishes, such as soups, casseroles, salads, and stews. It is often paired with chicken and other poultry, lamb, pork, steaks, and fish, especially oily fish. It also goes well with grains, mushrooms, onions, peas, potatoes, and spinach.

Rosemary Sweet Potato Fries

Ingredients

3 tablespoons olive oil
1 tablespoon minced fresh rosemary
1 garlic clove, minced
1 teaspoon cornstarch
3/4 teaspoon salt
1/8 teaspoon pepper
3 large sweet potatoes, peeled and cut into 1/4-inch julienned strips (about 2-1/4 pounds)

Instructions

- Preheat oven to 425°. In a large resealable plastic bag, combine the first six ingredients. Add sweet potatoes; shake to coat.
- Arrange in a single layer on two 15x10x1-in. baking pans coated with cooking spray. Bake, uncovered, 30-35 minutes or until tender and lightly browned, turning occasionally.

Rosemary and Butternut Lasagne

Ingredients
9 uncooked whole grain lasagne noodles
1 medium butternut squash (about 3 pounds), peeled and cut crosswise into 1/4-inch slices
2 tablespoons olive oil
1 teaspoon salt, divided
6 tablespoons all-purpose flour
4 cups fat-free milk
6 garlic cloves, minced
1 tablespoon minced fresh rosemary
1-1/3 cups shredded Parmesan cheese

Instructions
- Preheat oven to 425°. Cook noodles according to package directions; drain.
- In a large bowl, combine squash, oil and 1/2 teaspoon salt; toss to coat. Transfer to a 15x10x1-in. baking pan coated with cooking spray. Bake 10-15 minutes or until tender; remove from oven. Reduce heat to 375°.
- Place flour and remaining salt in a large saucepan; gradually whisk in milk. Bring to a boil, stirring constantly. Cook and stir 1-2 minutes or until thickened. Stir in garlic and rosemary.
- Spread 1 cup sauce into a 13x9-in. baking dish coated with cooking spray. Layer with three noodles, 1/3 cup cheese, a third of the squash and 1 cup sauce. Repeat layers twice. Sprinkle with remaining cheese.
- Cover and bake 40 minutes. Uncover; bake 10 minutes or until bubbly and top is lightly browned. Let stand 10 minutes before serving.

Notes

7. Chives

Chives are a perennial member of the onion family that sport beautiful edible flowers. Plus, they're a wonderful companion plant that helps deter pests.

Chives add a mild onion-like flavouring to dishes. People tend to use chives as a garnish or topping for main meals or salads, though they can also substitute chives for onions in other recipes. Chives are a common topping for foods such as: omelettes.

The two species of chives commonly grown in home gardens are common chives (Allium schoenoprasum) and garlic chives (A. tuberosum).

Cheese and chive scones

Ingredients
450g/1lb self-raising flour, plus extra for dusting
2 tsp baking powder
pinch salt
1 tsp English mustard powder
50g/1¾oz butter, cubed
225g/8oz mature cheddar, grated
bunch chives, chopped
200-250ml/7-9fl oz milk

Instructions
- Preheat the oven to 210C/190C Fan/Gas 6½.
- Sift the flour, baking powder, salt and mustard powder into a large bowl. Using your fingertips, rub in the butter until the mix resembles fine crumbs. Stir in about 200g/7oz of the cheese, and the chives. Add enough of the milk to bring the mixture together to a soft, but not sticky, dough.
- Turn out the dough onto a lightly floured surface and briefly knead. Roll out the dough to about 4cm/1½in thick. Using a 6-7cm/2½-2¾in cookie cutter, cut out the scones and transfer to a baking sheet.
- Brush the tops with a little milk and sprinkle the remaining cheese over the scones. Bake for 12-15 minutes until well risen and golden.
- Cool on a wire rack. Serve while still slightly warm. Cut in half and top each with a slice of cheese, a slice of pear and a drizzle of honey.

Chive Egg muffins

Ingredients
6 slices streaky bacon
6 large or 7 medium eggs
100g / 1.5 cups cheddar cheese
1 tbsp chopped fresh chives
1 tsp dried mixed herbs
pepper to taste

Instructions
- Preheat the oven to 175c / 350f. Fill each hole in a 6-hole muffin tin with a square of parchment paper.

- Line each of the holes in the muffin tin with a slice of streaky bacon and bake in the oven for 10 minutes.

- In a large jug crack in the eggs and whisk with a fork. Add the cheese, dried and fresh herbs and pepper and mix again. Pour the egg mixture into the muffin holes on top of the bacon, dividing equally between each.

- Bake for 20-25 minutes until the muffins are cooked and firm and starting to brown on top.

- Serve immediately or allow to cool and store in the fridge for up to 3 days in an airtight container.

Notes

8. Garlic Chives

Garlic chives (also called Chinese chives) look similar to common chives, but their leaves are flatter, greener, and get to be about 20 inches in height. As their name suggests, their leaves have a mild garlic flavour (bulbs are more intense). Flowers are white and are larger and less densely clustered than those of common chives.

It's not just the leaves you can eat, though -- the flower stems, buds, and white blossoms are all edible too. (Sometimes different varieties are grown for their leaves and others for their flower stems, but both can be harvested from the same plant.)

Garlic chives can be chopped and used as a garnish just like regular chives are; try using them in compound butter or sprinkling on soup.

Garlic Chive Butter

Ingredients
1 pound (4 sticks) unsalted butter
1/2 cup finely chopped fresh garlic chives

Instructions

- In a large bowl, mash butter with a potato masher or just squish with hands. You can even cream butter using paddle attachment of a stand mixer—the goal is to get the butter soft enough to be able to incorporate garlic chives.

- Add chopped garlic chives and continue mashing/squishing/mixing butter until fully mixed.

- Spread out a large (1-foot or bigger) square of plastic wrap across work surface, then scoop mixed butter onto plastic. You are now going to roll the butter into a cylinder inside the plastic wrap

- Tie excess plastic wrap at ends of the cylinder into a knot, or just use little pieces of string to tie off the ends. You can even make a string out of a short section of plastic wrap and roll it into a little rope.

- Chill or freeze until needed.

Pork and Garlic Chive Stir Fry

Ingredients
Pork & marinade
8 oz (225 g) pork loin (or chop), sliced into thin strips
1/4 teaspoon sugar
2 teaspoons dark soy sauce
2 teaspoons Shaoxing wine (or dry sherry)
2 teaspoons cornstarch
Sauce
1 tablespoon water
1 teaspoon dark soy sauce
1/2 teaspoon chicken bouillon powder
1/2 teaspoon sugar
Stir Fry
1 tablespoon peanut oil
1" (2.5 cm) ginger , minced
4 Thai chilis , chopped (or 1 small jalapeno, diced)
8 oz (225 g) garlic chive , chopped into 2" (5 cm) pieces

Instructions
- Add the pork with the sugar, dark soy, and wine in a small bowl. Mix until the liquid is absorbed. Add the cornstarch and mix again. Marinate for 15 minutes while preparing the rest of the ingredients.
- Combine the sauce ingredients in a small bowl and set aside.
- Heat a large skillet with peanut oil over medium high heat until hot. Spread out the marinated pork to the pan with as little overlapping as possible. Cook undisturbed for 30 seconds, or until the bottom is cooked. Flip the pork. Immediately add the ginger, Thai chilis, and garlic sprouts. Continue stir and cook for 1 minute.
- Pour the sauce into the pan. Stir and cook until the sauce is reduced and coated to all the ingredients. Immediately transfer everything to a serving plate to prevent overcooking.
- Serve hot over rice as a part of a multi-course meal or as a light main dish

Notes

9. Lavender

Lavender is an herb native to northern Africa and the mountainous regions of the Mediterranean. Lavender is also grown for the production of its essential oil.

Lavender pairs really well with rich and fatty foods because it cuts through and lifts the overall flavour. Lavender is often paired with chicken, turkey, lamb, and fatty fish like salmon or tuna.

Lavender leaves are edible and very strongly flavoured. English Lavender has the sweetest fragrance and is great for cooking.

Lemon Lavender Avocado Loaf

Ingredients

2 ⅔ cups all-purpose flour
1 ½ teaspoons baking soda
1 teaspoon baking powder
¾ teaspoon salt
½ cup butter, softened
1 ¾ cups white sugar
3 eggs
1 ½ cups mashed avocado
2 tablespoons lemon juice
¾ cup milk
2 tablespoons dried lavender
1 tablespoon grated lemon zest

Instructions

- Preheat an oven to 350 degrees F (175 degrees C). Grease and flour 2 9x5 inch loaf pans.
- Mix flour, baking soda, baking powder, and salt in a bowl. Set aside. Beat the butter and sugar with an electric mixer in a large bowl until light and fluffy. The mixture should be noticeably lighter in colour. Add the room-temperature eggs one at a time, allowing each egg to blend into the butter mixture before adding the next. Beat in the avocado and lemon juice with the last egg. Pour in the flour mixture alternately with the milk, mixing until just incorporated. Fold in the lavender and lemon zest; mixing just enough to evenly combine. Pour the batter into prepared pans.
- Bake in the preheated oven until a toothpick inserted into the centre comes out clean, about 1 hour. Cool in the pans for 10 minutes before removing to cool completely on a wire rack.

Lavender Truffles

Ingredients

12 fresh lavender flower heads
⅓ cup heavy cream
6 ounces bittersweet chocolate, chopped
4 ounces semisweet chocolate, chopped
2 tablespoons unsalted butter

Instructions

- Place the flower heads and cream into a small microwave safe glass bowl. Cook in the microwave on High until hot to the touch, 20 to 30 seconds. Once hot, stir the flowers with a spoon, and set aside to steep 5 minutes. Return to the microwave and cook 10 to 20 seconds to reheat. Stir again and set aside to steep 5 minutes more. Repeat the heating-stirring-steeping process two more times until the cream is strongly flavoured with lavender.
- Combine the bittersweet chocolate with the semisweet chocolate in a microwave safe glass bowl. Divide the chocolate into equal portions and set one portion aside. Cook the remaining chocolate in the microwave on High in 20 to 30 second increments until melted, stirring between each heating. Using a fine-mesh strainer, strain the cream into the melted chocolate; discard the flower heads and bits of lavender. Stir the cream and chocolate together until smooth. Chill in the refrigerator until somewhat firm, but not hard, about 1 hour.
- After the lavender chocolate mixture has chilled, place the remaining chocolate and butter into a microwave safe glass bowl. Cook in the microwave on High in 20 to 30 second increments until just melted, stirring between each heating; set aside.
- Line a baking sheet with a piece of waxed paper. Roll the lavender mixture into 1 tablespoon-sized balls, and dip into the melted chocolate mixture using a skewer or toothpick. Place onto the prepared baking sheet, and chill in the refrigerator at least 2 hours to harden.

Notes

10. Marjoram

Marjoram, also known as sweet marjoram, is an aromatic herb in the mint family that has been grown in the Mediterranean, North Africa, and Western Asia for thousands of years.

While similar to oregano, it has a milder flavour and is often used to garnish salads, soups, and meat dishes.

Mushroom Crostini

Ingredients
8 tbsp olive oil
2 garlic cloves, 1 peeled, 1 finely chopped
1 small red chilli, finely chopped
400g/14oz mixed mushrooms, chopped
1 tbsp coarsely chopped fresh flatleaf parsley
1 tbsp fresh marjoram leaves
salt and freshly ground black pepper
8 slices Pugliese (or sourdough) bread

Instructions
- Heat six tablespoons of the olive oil in a frying pan, fry the chopped garlic and chilli for one minute, then add the mushrooms and fry for a further 2-3 minutes, or until cooked.

- Stir in the parsley and marjoram and season with salt and freshly ground black pepper.

- Meanwhile, toast the slices of bread on both sides. Rub each piece of bread lightly with the whole garlic clove and brush with the remaining olive oil, then slice into individual servings if needed. Spoon over the mushrooms and serve.

Red Cabbage stir-fry with Marjoram, Pecans and Blue Cheese

Ingredients
75g/2½oz pecans
pinch cayenne pepper
3 tbsp olive oil
3 tbsp balsamic vinegar, plus more if needed
1 red onion, thinly sliced
1 garlic clove, finely chopped
1 small red cabbage, finely shredded
pinch brown sugar, plus more if needed
100g/3½ oz blue cheese, crumbled/diced
2 apples, peeled and finely diced
2 tbsp chopped parsley
2 tsp chopped marjoram
salt and freshly ground black pepper

Instructions
- Preheat the oven to 200C/180C Fan/Gas 6.
- Toss the pecans in salt and the cayenne pepper. Place on a baking tray and cook in the preheated oven for 5 minutes, or until lightly toasted.
- Put the oil and vinegar in a large saucepan over a medium heat. Add the onion and garlic and cook for a few minutes, stirring regularly. Tip in the cabbage and stir fry together for a few more minutes, or until the colour changes and the cabbage wilts. Season with salt and pepper really well, adding a little sugar and more vinegar if needed.
- Finally add the cheese, apple, herbs and toasted nuts. Toss together and serve.

Notes

11. Origanum

Origanum means 'Joy of the Mountain', a fitting name for a herb that was traditionally grown on the hills of the Mediterranean. Oregano is easily confused with its close relative, marjoram.

Some of the most common uses of oregano include tomato-centric recipes, like pizza and pasta sauce, as well as olive oil-based dishes. Oregano is commonly combined with olive oil to create flavourful oregano oil, Italian vinaigrettes, and marinades for lamb, chicken, and beef dishes. Other ingredients that pair well with oregano include garlic, basil, onion, and thyme.

Fresh Oregano Pesto

Ingredients
1 cup fresh oregano, tightly packed
1/2 cup grated parmesan cheese
2 cloves garlic, peeled
1/2 cup raw almonds
salt and pepper to taste
1/2 cup olive oil

Instructions

- Add all ingredients but the olive oil to the bowl of a food processor and grind until the mixture is slightly combined.

- With the processor still running, slowly stream in the olive oil until the mixture becomes smooth.

- Store in an airtight container in the fridge, or freeze for later use (see notes for tips)

Notes:
To store: pop the pesto into the fridge for around 5-7 days. I usually put an extra little layer of olive oil on top of the pesto, and it helps to preserve it for a little longer and stops it from going brown on top.
If you want to freeze it then I usually freeze my pesto in ice cube trays. Just pop the mixture into the ice cube tray, freeze, and once frozen remove and store in a ziploc bag until needed.

Yellow Squash and Zucchini Pasta Salad with Fresh Oregano

Ingredients

16 ounces farfalle (bowtie) pasta
1 pound yellow summer (crookneck) squash, cut into 1-in. chunks
1 pound zucchini, halved lengthwise and cut into 1-in. chunks
1/2 cup olive oil, divided
Salt
2 tablespoons Champagne vinegar
About 1/2 tsp. freshly ground black pepper
2 tablespoons chopped fresh oregano
1/4 to 1/2 cup toasted pine nuts
1/4 cup chopped pitted kalamata olives

Instructions

- Cook pasta in a large pot of boiling salted water until tender to the bite, 9 to 12 minutes or according to package directions. Drain and rinse thoroughly under cold water until completely cool.
- Prepare a gas or charcoal grill for medium heat (you can hold your hand 5 in. above cooking grate only 5 to 7 seconds). Thread squash and zucchini chunks onto 10- to 12-in. metal skewers and place on a baking sheet. Brush vegetables with 1/4 to 1/3 cup olive oil on all sides and sprinkle with salt to taste. Transfer to grill and cook 10 to 15 minutes, turning occasionally, or until vegetables are very tender.
- Meanwhile, whisk together remaining olive oil, the vinegar, and 1/2 tsp. pepper in a small bowl.
- With a fork, push vegetables off skewers back onto baking sheet and toss them in oil left there. In a large bowl, toss together pasta, vegetables, oregano, pine nuts, and olives. Add dressing and salt and pepper to taste; toss.
- Serve warm or cold.

Notes

12. Thyme

Thyme is the herb of some members of the genus Thymus of aromatic perennial evergreen herbs in the mint family Lamiaceae. Thymes are relatives of the oregano genus Origanum, with both plants being mostly indigenous to the Mediterranean region.

Thyme (fresh and dried) pairs well with meats of all kinds, chicken, stews, soups, eggs, pastas, vegetables, and beans. Fresh thyme is nice with fish and seafood. Think of thyme when you are making lasagne, sautéing or roasting vegetables, roasting chicken, pork, lamb, or beef, and making any sort of potato dish.

Lemon and Thyme Pork Schnitzel

Ingredients

2 x 180g/6oz pork loin steaks, fat trimmed
salt and freshly ground black pepper
1 large free-range egg
2 tbsp plain flour
75g/2½oz coarse dried white breadcrumbs, preferably Japanese panko breadcrumbs
½ lemon, zest only, finely grated
15g/½oz parmesan, finely grated
1 heaped tbsp chopped fresh thyme leaves
300ml/10½fl oz sunflower oil

Instructions

- For the pork schnitzels, sandwich one of the pork loin steaks between two sheets of cling film. Flatten the steak using a rolling pin or meat mallet to an even thickness of 1cm/½in. Remove the cling film and cut the flattened steak in half lengthways. Season on both sides with salt and freshly ground black pepper. Repeat the process with the remaining pork loin steaks.
- Beat the egg in a bowl. Sprinkle the flour onto a plate. Mix the breadcrumbs, lemon zest, parmesan, thyme and a good pinch of salt in a shallow bowl until well combined.
- Dredge each piece of pork first into the flour, then dip it into the beaten egg, then dredge it in the breadcrumb mixture until completely coated. Repeat the process with the remaining pieces of pork.
- Heat the sunflower oil in a large frying pan until a breadcrumb sizzles and turns golden-brown when dropped into it. (Caution: hot oil can be dangerous. Do not leave unattended.)
- Add two of the schnitzels to the pan and fry for 2-3 minutes on each side, or until the pork is cooked through and the coating is crisp and golden-brown. Remove from the pan using a pair of tongs and set aside to drain on a warmed plate lined with kitchen paper. Keep warm. Repeat the process with the remaining two pork schnitzels.

Stuffed Marrow with Thyme

Ingredients

1 medium marrow, cut in half widthways
5 garlic cloves
3 tbsp chopped fresh thyme
3 tbsp olive oil, plus extra for brushing the marrow
2 large onions, roughly chopped
500g/1lb 2oz beef mince
2 tbsp tomato purée
2 tbsp sun-dried tomato paste (or 2 tbsp chopped sundried tomatoes)
450g/1lb fresh tomatoes (or 1 x 400g/14oz can chopped tomatoes)
3 tbsp finely chopped fresh parsley, plus extra for serving
3 free-range eggs, beaten
75g/2¼oz parmesan, grated, plus extra for serving
75g pecorino, grated
salt and freshly ground black pepper

Instructions

- Preheat the oven to 180C/350F/Gas 4. Line a large roasting tin with foil.
- Bring a large pan of water to the boil and season the water lightly with salt.
- Scoop the seeds and about 120g/4½oz of the flesh from the inside of the marrow, creating a large hollow, and put to one side. Carefully lower the hollowed marrow halves into the pan of boiling water, immediately turn the heat off and leave them sitting in the hot water until you are ready to use them.
- Crush the garlic and fresh thyme in a pestle and mortar and add salt and freshly ground pepper to taste. Heat the olive oil in a pan, add the onions, followed by the garlic and thyme, and then fry until soft. Add the beef mince and cook for about 10 minutes, stirring regularly until browned.
- Chop the peeled tomatoes roughly and add the tomato purée and sun-dried tomato paste to the browned beef mince and cook for another 5 minutes. Chop the reserved flesh from the marrow and stir it into the sauce, stir in the parsley and cook for a further 10 minutes, stirring occasionally.
- Take the sauce off the heat and let it cool briefly before stirring in the eggs (if the eggs are stirred in too soon they will scramble).
- Add half of the parmesan and pecorino to the pan and stir until well combined.
- Carefully remove the 2 halves of marrow from the hot water, draining any water from the centre, and place them in the baking tin. Spoon the sauce mixture into each of the marrow halves until they are full. Gently push the halves together and brush the skin with olive oil. Sprinkle the remaining half of the grated cheeses over the top of the marrow. Wrap the sides of the foil around the marrow to hold it together, leaving a small gap at the top.
- Bake in the preheated oven for about 45 minutes. After 45 minutes, increase the temperature to 200C/400F/Gas 6, open out the foil and cook for another 5 minutes so the grated cheese can brown and become crispy. Remove from the oven and allow to rest for 10 minutes.
- To serve, slice the marrow into rings, and sprinkle with extra parmesan and parsley to serve, if you like.

Notes

13. Mint

Mint is a perennial herb with very fragrant, toothed leaves and tiny purple, pink, or white flowers. There are many varieties of mint—all fragrant, whether shiny or fuzzy, smooth or crinkled, bright green or variegated.

Fresh mint leaves are usually cut in ribbons (chiffonade) and added to recipes. A stalk with a few tender leaves is placed in a hot or cold beverage and may be crushed (muddled) to release more flavour. Dried mint leaves can be added to a sauce or stew as it simmers.

Serious cooks generally prefer spearmint for savory dishes and peppermint for desserts. For a delicate mint taste in fruit salads, yogurt, or tea, try apple or orange mint.

Steamed Trout with Mint & Dill Dressing

Ingredients

120g new potatoes, halved
170g pack asparagus spears, woody ends trimmed
1 ½ tsp vegetable bouillon powder made up to 225ml with water
80g fine green beans, trimmed
80g frozen peas
2 skinless trout fillets
2 slices lemon
For the dressing
4 tbsp bio yogurt
1 tsp cider vinegar
¼ tsp English mustard powder
1 tsp finely chopped mint
2 tsp chopped dill

Instructions

- Put the new potatoes on to simmer in a pan of boiling water until tender. Cut the asparagus in half to shorten the spears and slice the ends without the tips. Tip the bouillon into a wide non-stick pan. Add the asparagus and beans, then cover and cook for 5 mins.
-
- Add the peas to the pan, then top with the trout and lemon slices. Cover again and cook for 5 mins more until the fish flakes really easily but is still juicy.
-
- Meanwhile, mix the yogurt with the vinegar, mustard powder, mint and dill. Stir in 2-3 tbsp of the fish cooking juices. Put the veg and any remaining pan juices in bowls, top with the fish and herb dressing, then serve with the potatoes.

Pea & Mint Soup

Ingredients

1 bunch spring onions, trimmed and roughly chopped
1 medium potato, peeled and diced
1 garlic clove, crushed
850ml vegetable or chicken stock
900g young pea in the pod (to give about 250g/9oz shelled peas)
4tbsp chopped fresh mint
large pinch caster sugar
1 tbsp fresh lemon or lime juice
150ml buttermilk or soured cream

Instructions

- Put the spring onions into a large pan with the potato, garlic and stock. Bring to the boil, turn down the heat and simmer for 15 minutes or until the potato is very soft. For the garnish, blanch 3 tbsp of the shelled peas in boiling water for 2-3 minutes, drain, put in a bowl of cold water and set aside. Add the remaining peas to the soup base and simmer for 5 minutes – no longer, or you will lose the lovely fresh flavour of the peas.
- Stir in the mint, sugar and lemon or lime juice, cool slightly then pour into a food processor or liquidiser and whizz until as smooth as you like. Stir in half the buttermilk or soured cream, taste and season with salt and pepper.
- To serve the soup cold, cool quickly, then chill – you may need to add more stock to the soup before serving as it will thicken as it cools. To serve hot, return the soup to the rinsed-out pan and reheat without boiling (to prevent the buttermilk or soured cream from curdling).
- Serve the soup in bowls, garnished with the remaining buttermilk and the drained peas.

Notes

14. Sage

Garden or common sage (Salvia officinalis) is the most common type of sage used for cooking.

Frying a strong herb like sage mellows its flavour. Fried sage can be crumbled over a dish to heighten flavour at the last moment. Sage can also be used to add herbaceousness to sauces, compound butters, meat marinades, pastries, and breads. Add fresh sage leaves to cocktails and teas for an instant hit of herbal flavour.

Popular in both Italian and British cookery, sage has long, grey-green leaves with a slightly furry surface. Its aroma is pungent, and it has a strong, slightly minty, musky taste. Traditionally, it's used to flavour sausages and as a stuffing for fatty meats such as pork and goose.

Creamy Squash and Sage Gratin

Ingredients
double cream 300ml
whole milk 150ml
Dijon mustard 1 tsp
dried chilli flakes a pinch
garlic 1 clove, crushed
sage a small handful of leaves, chopped
butternut squash 1kg, peeled, deseeded, and thinly sliced

Instructions
- Heat the oven to 190C/fan 170C/gas 5. Put all the ingredients except the squash in a small pan, season really well and bring to just below boiling point.
- Arrange the squash slices in a shallow ovenproof dish and pour over the infused cream.
- Bake for 30-40 minutes (press the squash down with a spatula halfway through cooking) or until the squash is tender and the top pale golden and bubbling.
- Leave the gratin to sit for 10 minutes before serving.

Grilled Fontina, Mushroom, and Sage Sandwiches

Ingredients
3 tablespoons butter, 2 melted
1/2 pound mushrooms, cut into thin slices
1/4 teaspoon salt
1/8 teaspoon fresh-ground black pepper
4 teaspoons chopped fresh sage, or 1 1/4 teaspoons dried sage
8 slices from a large round loaf of country-style bread, or other bread
1/2 pound fontina, grated (about 2 cups)

Instructions
- In a large non-stick frying pan, heat 1 tablespoon of the butter over moderate heat. Add the mushrooms, salt, pepper, and dried sage, if using, and cook, stirring frequently, until golden brown, about 5 minutes. Stir in the fresh sage, if using. Put the mushrooms in a bowl and wipe out the pan.
- Using a pastry brush, coat one side of 4 slices of the bread with half of the melted butter. Put them, buttered-side down, on a work surface. Top the bread with the cheese and then the mushrooms. Cover with the remaining 4 slices of bread; brush the tops with the remaining melted butter.
- Heat the frying pan over moderately low heat. Add the sandwiches and cook, turning once, until golden, about 2 minutes per side.

Notes

15. Tarragon

Tarragon, also known as estragon, is a species of perennial herb in the sunflower family. It is a culinary herb that is known for its glossy, skinny leaves and aromatic flavour.

Tarragon is a leafy green herb that is highly aromatic with a subtle liquorice flavour. It adds a fresh, spring taste and a bit of elegance to a variety of recipes, including salad dressings, sauces, and fish and chicken dishes, and is commonly used in French cooking.

Fishcakes with Herb Salad

Ingredients

For the marinade
½ garlic clove, chopped
2 tbsp olive oil
1 tsp salt
1 tbsp lilliput capers
1 tbsp chopped fresh dill

For the fishcakes
50g/1¾oz sea bass, skin removed and diced
50g/1¾oz natural smoked haddock, skin removed and diced
50g/1¾oz salmon, skin removed and diced
100g/3½oz mashed potato

For the coating
150g/5½oz plain flour
150g/5½oz panko breadcrumbs

For the herb dressing
1 free-range egg yolk
½ garlic clove
1 tbsp white wine vinegar
1 tbsp Dijon mustard
pinch sugar
1 tbsp chopped fresh tarragon
1 tbsp chopped fresh dill
1 tbsp chopped fresh flatleaf parsley
1 handful rocket leaves
50ml/2fl oz extra virgin olive oil
100ml/3½fl oz vegetable oil

To serve
1 tbsp fresh tarragon, chopped
1 tbsp fresh dill, chopped
1 tbsp flatleaf parsley, chopped
2 nasturtium flowers, petals picked, and 6 nasturtium leaves
2 tbsp capers

Instructions
- To make the marinade, place all the ingredients in a bowl and mix to combine. To make the fishcakes, add the sea bass, haddock, and salmon to the bowl of marinade, stir to coat thoroughly and leave whilst you prepare the rest of the ingredients.

- Preheat a deep fat fryer to 180C. Mix the fish and marinade with the mashed potato and shape into two flattened fishcakes.

- To coat the fishcakes, put 50g/1¾oz of the plain flour and a pinch of salt in a shallow bowl and mix in about 100ml/3½fl oz water to create a batter consistency. Put the remaining flour in another bowl, and the breadcrumbs in another. Dip the fishcakes in the flour first, then the batter and finally the breadcrumbs. Deep-fry the fishcakes for 4–5 minutes until golden on the outside and hot inside.

- To make the dressing, blitz all the dressing ingredients, except the oil, in a food processor, then slowly pour in both oils with the processor running until combined.

- Place the fishcakes onto two serving plates, then top with the herbs, petals, leaves, capers, and dressing.

Creamy Chicken Pie with Tarragon

Ingredients
1 tbsp sunflower oil
3 boneless, skinless chicken breasts (around 500g/1lb 2oz), cut into roughly 2cm/¾in chunks
1 onion, finely chopped
300g/10½oz chestnut mushrooms, halved or quartered if large
4 tsp plain flour
1 tsp garlic powder or 1 garlic clove, crushed
1 tsp dried tarragon
400ml/14fl oz chicken stock, made with 1 stock cube
4 tbsp reduced fat crème fraîche
2 x sheets filo pastry (around 85g/3oz)
freshly ground black pepper

Instructions
- Place a baking tray in the oven and preheat the oven to 220C/200C Fan/Gas 7.
- Brush a large, deep non-stick frying pan with a little of the oil and place over a high heat. Add the chicken pieces, season with freshly ground black pepper and stir-fry for 3 minutes over a high heat, or until lightly coloured on all sides. Transfer to a plate.
- Return the pan to the heat, brush with a little more oil (make sure to use a heatproof silicone pastry brush). Fry the onion and mushrooms over a high heat for about 5 minutes, or until lightly browned.
- Sprinkle over the flour, garlic and tarragon and stir well. Gradually add the stock, just a little at a time, stirring constantly until the sauce is thickened.
- Stir in the crème fraîche and return the chicken to the pan. Adjust the seasoning to taste and spoon into a warmed 1 litre/1¾ pint pie dish (see Recipe Tip).
- Cut each pastry sheet into three wide strips and brush lightly with the remaining sunflower oil. Scrunch each sheet loosely and place layered on top of the pie filling. Bake on the baking tray in the centre of the oven for 10–12 minutes, or until the pastry is golden-brown and the filling is bubbling. Serve.

List of Recipes

		Page
1.	Potato Salad with Dill	6
2.	Dill Pickles	7
3.	Creamy Pasta with Fennel, Spring Onions, and Bacon	10
4.	Fennel Frond Pesto with Anchovies	11
5.	Pomegranate and Parsley Salad	14
6.	Easy Potato Tortilla with Parsley and Chorizo	15
7.	Green chutney	18
8.	Lemon and coriander couscous	19
9.	Basil and Lentil Salad	22
10.	Tuna and Green Bean Salad with Basil Dressing	23
11.	Rosemary Sweet Potato Fries	
12.	Rosemary and Butternut Lasagne	26
13.	Cheese and chive scones	27
14.	Chive Egg muffins	30
15.	Garlic Chive Butter	31
16.	Pork and Garlic Chive Stir Fry	34
17.	Lemon Lavender Avocado Loaf	35
18.	Lavender Truffles	38
19.	Mushroom Crostini	39
20.	Red Cabbage stir-fry with Marjoram, Pecans and Blue Cheese	42
21.	Fresh Oregano Pesto	43
22.	Yellow Squash and Zucchini Pasta Salad with Fresh Oregano	46
23.	Lemon and Thyme Pork Schnitzel	47
24.	Stuffed Marrow with Thyme	50
25.	Steamed Trout with Mint & Dill Dressing	51
26.	Pea & Mint Soup	54
27.	Creamy Squash and Sage Gratin	55
28.	Grilled Fontina, Mushroom, and Sage Sandwiches	58
29.	Creamy Chicken Pie with Tarragon	59
30.	Fishcakes with Herb Salad	62
		64

Notes

Notes

Notes

Notes

Notes